Hunting
DEER

Hines Lambert

PowerKiDS
press

New York

Published in 2013 by The Rosen Publishing Group, Inc.
29 East 21st Street, New York, NY 10010

First Edition

Editor: Amelie von Zumbusch
Book Design: Kate Laczynski

Photo Credits: Background graphic © iStockphoto.com/Andrea Zanchi; sidebar binoculars © iStockphoto.com/ Feng Yu; cover Mike Rogal/Shutterstock.com; pp. 4, 22 MCT/McClatchy-Tribune/Getty Images; p. 5 Bruce MacQueen/Shutterstock.com; p. 6 DCDacis/Flickr/Getty Images; pp. 7, 9 (right) B.G. Smith/Shutterstock.com; p. 8 eans/Shutterstock.com; pp. 9 (left), 21 iStockphoto/Thinkstock; p. 10 Ian Spanier/Aurora+/Getty Images; p. 11 Roger Pilkington/Shutterstock.com; p. 12 David Nevala/Aurora/Getty Images; p. 13 Mark Hirsch/ WireImage/Getty Images; p. 15 Guy J. Sagi/Shutterstock.com; p. 16 Konjushenko Vladimir/Shutterstock.com; p. 17 (left) Fuse/Getty Images; pp. 17 (right), 23 Nate A./Shutterstock.com; p. 19 dcwcreations/Shutterstock. com; p. 20 Steve Liss/Time & Life Images/Getty Images; p. 24 Kansas City Star/McClatchy-Tribune/Getty Images; p. 25 Jupiterimages/Comstock Images/Getty Images; p. 26 RubberBall Productions/the Agency Collection/Getty Images; p. 27 Jeremy Woodhouse/The Image Bank/Getty Images; p. 28 Darryl Brooks/ Shutterstock.com; p. 29 Wichita Eagle/McClatchy/Getty Images.

Library of Congress Cataloging-in-Publication Data

Lambert, Hines.
  Hunting deer / by Hines Lambert. — 1st ed.
    p. cm. — (Let's go hunting)
  Includes index.
  ISBN 978-1-4488-9659-2 (library binding) — ISBN 978-1-4488-9776-6 (pbk.) —
  ISBN 978-1-4488-9777-3 (6-pack)
  1. Deer hunting—Juvenile literature. I. Title.
  SK301.L36 2013
  799.2'765—dc23
                                      2012023214

Manufactured in the United States of America

CPSIA Compliance Information: Batch #W13PK2: For Further Information contact Rosen Publishing, New York, New York at 1-800-237-9932

CONTENTS

Millions of Americans enjoy the great outdoors every year. Some go camping, boating, or even mountain climbing. Deer hunting is another way to enjoy the great outdoors. Many people believe that hunters do not care for animals and nature. This is not true. Most hunters admire the beauty of the animals they hunt. Hunters believe they are part of nature. Animals kill other

Deer hunting is an activity that many families enjoy doing together.

A single deer supplies a lot of meat. Meat from an animal that has been hunted is often healthier than meat from a store.

animals in order to survive. Hunters are part of this process.

Some hunters might also point out that most Americans eat meat bought at a store. Someone had to kill that animal before it ended up on a shelf in the market. Deer hunters argue that they earned the right to eat their kills because hunting deer provides a challenge.

The United States is home to dozens of kinds of deer. All of these deer belong to two main **species**. These are the white-tailed deer and the mule deer. Scientists break these two species down into subspecies. For example, Columbian black-tailed deer are a kind of mule deer.

Even though both white-tailed deer and mule deer are native to North America, they did not always live

You can recognize a white-tailed deer because the underside of its tail is white. These deer are found in 48 states.

Mule deer, such as this one, are bigger than white-tailed deer.

here. There was a time when there were no deer in North America at all! The first deer came from very far away, in a place now called Mongolia. Millions of years ago, these deer journeyed across a land bridge to reach the places we now call Alaska and Canada. Today, about 20 million deer live in the United States.

Did You Know?

The fur of the white-tailed deer changes color over the year. It is more reddish brown in the spring and summer, but it changes to gray brown in the fall and winter.

Some hunters prefer to be on the move while they hunt. They usually practice still-hunting or spot-and-stalk hunting. Still-hunting is not at all what it sounds like. Still-hunters do not sit still! They move a lot. Still-hunters move silently and slowly. They have to be in good shape. It is called still-hunting because they move so slowly that it appears to deer that they are still. This is important because deer see movement very easily.

Spot-and-stalk hunters need to be very quiet to sneak up on a deer.

It is easier to stalk deer in the snow because you can follow their tracks, or footprints.

Deer can be hard to see because their coats often blend in with the woods and fields where they live.

Spot-and-stalk hunters do not sit still either. They stalk deer until they are close enough to shoot. Good stalkers know how to spot and follow deer tracks. They must walk quietly and carefully. Deer will run away if a hunter steps on a twig. Good stalkers also know to stand downwind because deer will avoid the smell of humans.

9

Drives and Dogs

Hunters must plan ahead and work together well to have success on a deer drive.

A deer drive is a popular way to hunt with a group. Hunters working a deer drive think of themselves as members of a team. If a hunter shoots a deer, the entire team wins. Some members of the team stay in specific spots all day. These hunters might be the best shots in the group. Other hunters will walk through the woods and "drive" the deer toward the hunters who stayed put.

Some states allow deer hunters to bring along dogs. Dogs can smell and hear much better than humans, so they make great hunters. It is important that your dog be well behaved. Dogs should never chase deer. This could spoil someone else's hunt. Your dog could also get shot!

Scottish deerhounds were originally bred to hunt deer.

Deer have strong senses of sight, smell, and hearing. They also run very fast. This makes them hard to kill! Humans have been hunting deer for thousands of years. Over all that time, we have learned ways to outsmart them.

Still-hunters often use **tree stands** to avoid being seen. Tree stands often look like simple tree houses. Some tree stands are simply chairs attached to trees.

This deer hunter is using a hunting blind with a camouflage pattern.

Hunters in tree stands are less likely to be seen by deer. Since they are up high, they can see farther, too.

Hunters also use **blinds** to disappear. Blinds act as **camouflage** so that hunters can blend into their surroundings. Blinds are available in stores. Some look like tents or cabins. Hunters also make their own blinds out of sticks and leaves.

Did You Kno

Although deer can see fe~ colors than humans, they see better than us in low ~ such as in twilight or at d~

Food for Thought

Good hunters want deer to be healthy and strong. They can help deer by planting food plots. Food plots have plants that deer love. The plants that work best are often clovers, corn, and turnips.

Hunters who use food plots help all of the deer in the area. Food plots are good for the deer and for the hunter. Chances are good that a hunter who uses food plots will kill a big deer.

Many hunters do not have the land or the time to plant food plots. They can still attract deer by **baiting** them. You bait deer by placing food in a spot where you plan to hunt. Some states do not allow deer baiting. Many hunters believe hunting with bait is cheating.

Some people oppose feeding deer because it tends to bring big groups of deer together. This means sickness can spread more easily among the deer.

Most deer hunters use **rifles**. These are firearms that shoot single long bullets. Some rifles can shoot farther than 300 yards (274 m). That is farther than three football fields! Rifles are also very precise. A hunter who is a good shot is dangerous to deer.

Some hunters prefer to use **shotguns**. These do not shoot as far as rifles, but they can be powerful in short range. Hunters must load special shells called

Shotguns loaded with shells containing metal pellets, called shot, are used to hunt ducks and game birds. It is generally against the law to use these shells to hunt deer.

You need to be able to aim well to use a rifle.

slugs into shotguns in order to hunt deer. **Pistols** come in handy for hunting in deep brush and heavy forest. This is when a rifle might be too long and heavy. Pistols do not shoot as far as rifles. Make sure your firearm's **safety** is always on, and never point your firearm at anything unless you mean to shoot.

Some hunters prefer to hunt with bows because it presents an even greater challenge. Most bows are made from a special material called fiberglass. Fiberglass bows can be light. This makes it easier to stalk game. Some hunters use crossbows. These are special bows with triggers, just like guns. It takes a long time to reload crossbows, but they are powerful. Choosing the right arrow is just as important as choosing the right bow. Different arrows can be used for different animals.

Archery is a difficult skill to learn. It is important for bow hunters to practice and become expert shots. A firearm can shoot every time its chamber is loaded. It takes far longer to get another arrow ready. Good bow hunters make every shot count.

This deer hunter is using a compound bow. These bows use pulleys to make them more powerful.

Other Tools of the Trade

Have you ever mistaken a statue for a person? Deer can make the same mistake. Hunters often place deer statues, or decoys, to attract deer. Hunters can buy male or female decoys. Some hunters believe using a male, or buck, decoy is better for hunting males. A male deer will fight if it thinks another male wants to claim its area.

Other tools attract deer by making noise. These are calls or rattles. Calls sound like females. Some hunters

It is easy to mistake many decoys for real deer. Be careful when placing decoys. You do not want another hunter shooting at you!

Bucks use their antlers to fight during the mating season. Deer rattles make bucks think that other bucks are fighting nearby.

perform these sounds themselves, and others buy tools that make noises. A rattle sounds like the clicking of antlers. Some hunters use actual antlers as a rattle.

Hunters can also buy scents that attract deer. Think of these as perfume for deer! Scents can smell like the forest or like actual deer.

Did You Know?

In early America, the skin of a deer sold for about $1. This is why we call a dollar a buck.

It is important to see before you shoot. This is where **binoculars** and **scopes** come in. These are tools that help us see things that are far away. Scopes are often attached to rifles. Most scopes allow the hunter to see a target, or crosshairs, to help aim. Range finders are handy items because they tell hunters how far away an object is.

The thing on top of this young hunter's rifle is a scope.

These tools help hunters shoot, but they also help hunters decide when not to shoot. It is important to know what you are shooting at. Branches can often look like antlers. It might be illegal in your state to shoot at a deer without antlers. Always know for sure before you pull the trigger. Seeing clearly helps you be sure.

Before you go hunting, it is important to know your state's hunting laws and to have a hunting **license**. Just as a driver's license means you can safely drive a car, a hunting license means you know how to hunt safely. Hunting is dangerous only when people act carelessly.

Each state has different hunting laws that determine what time of year deer may be hunted, what weapons

States set rules for who can hunt when. These hunters are taking part in a deer hunt for young hunters and disabled hunters in Kansas.

If you have a junior license, you can learn a lot from the adult with whom you go hunting.

you may use, and how many deer you may kill. Most states require hunters to take a test in order to receive their hunting licenses. Young hunters may usually purchase junior licenses at the age of 12. A hunter with a junior license must hunt with an adult. You can find a list of hunting laws on your state's website.

Did You Know?

In the early 1900s, there were only about half a million white-tailed deer in the United States. Hunting laws came about to make sure this never happens again.

If a firearm can kill a deer, it can also kill a person. Never forget that you are carrying a dangerous weapon. Never shoot unless you are sure of your target. Make sure you see everything else that is near your target. What might you hit if you miss the deer?

The bright orange color that hunters wear for safety is often called hunter orange or blaze orange.

Never climb into a tree stand with a loaded gun. Remember to unload your firearm after your hunt. Always keep the safety on until you are ready to shoot. Never point your firearm at another person, even if the safety is on! It is best to treat your firearm as if it is always ready to shoot.

Most states require hunters to wear bright orange clothing. The human eye sees this color very well, but deer cannot.

Certain parts of a deer can be cut into venison steaks. These venison steaks are cooking on a grill.

You shot a deer. Now what? It is important to **field dress** your deer as soon as possible. This makes sure that the meat does not go bad. Deer meat is called venison, and it can be prepared in many ways. Hunters enjoy eating venison as steaks, jerky, sausage, or burgers. Organizations such as Hunters for the Hungry give venison away to hungry families.

Some hunters collect trophies. They might hang big sets of antlers or even stuffed deer heads on their walls. Good hunters are proud of their trophies, but they do not brag. They respect the deer and are thankful for them. Good hunters are aware of the part they play in the natural world.

Deer hunters are pr to take part in an a humans have done thousands of years

HUNTING TIPS

1 Even if it isn't deer season, you can still scout the woods to pick out hunting spots for next year!

2 Deer often move toward cover a day or so before a big storm. This is a great time to hunt.

3 You may be returning from your hunt after dark. Always bring a flashlight!

4 Don't spend all your time hunting in the same place. Try out different spots so that the deer cannot figure you out.

5 Spot-and-stalk hunting is easier on rainy days because it is harder for the deer to hear you.

6 Shower and wash your hunting clothes with scent-free soap so that the deer cannot smell you.

7 Check the direction of the wind by using a string tied to your weapon.

8 Be careful of loud sounds such as coughing and cell phones.

GLOSSARY

archery (**AHR-cheh-ree**) Shooting with a bow and arrow.

baiting (**BAYT-ing**) Using something to draw in animals being fished or hunted.

binoculars (**bih-NAH-kyuh-lurz**) Handheld lenses that make things seem closer.

blinds (**BLYNDZ**) Places where people hide to watch or shoot animals.

camouflage (**KA-muh-flahj**) A color or a pattern that matches the surroundings and helps hide something.

field dress (**FEELD DRES**) To remove the parts from a kill that would make the meat go bad.

license (**LY-suns**) Official permission to do something.

pistols (**PIS-tulz**) Small guns that are fired from the hand.

rifles (**RY-fulz**) Long guns that are fired from the shoulder.

safety (**SAYF-tee**) A part on a gun that keeps it from being fired by mistake.

scopes (**SKOHPS**) Metal tubes with lenses inside that hunters look through to make a target look larger.

shotguns (**SHOT-gunz**) Guns with smooth insides that are fired from the shoulder.

species (**SPEE-sheez**) One kind of living thing. All people are one species.

tree stands (**TREE STANDZ**) Seats or platforms that are fixed to trees for hunters to use.

INDEX

WEBSITES

Due to the changing nature of Internet links, PowerKids Press has developed an online list of websites related to the subject of this book. This site is updated regularly. Please use this link to access the list:
www.powerkidslinks.com/lgh/deer/